What They're Saying about *Every Excuse in the Book*

"You won't find an excuse for not laughing!"
> - Sergio Aragonés, premier
> *MAD Magazine* cartoonist

"I meant to come up with a blurb, but I've got the Epstein-Barr Syndrome."
> - Steve O'Donnell, former head writer,
> *Late Night with David Letterman*

(Note: We'd also hoped to get a quote from Elvis, but he's busy working double shifts at that donut shop in Schenectady.)

EVERY
Excuse
— in the —
BOOK

714 Ways to Say
"It's Not My Fault!"

Craig Boldman
and Pete Matthews
Pictures by the authors

MJF BOOKS
NEW YORK

To Our Parents,
who are totally responsible

Published by MJF Books
Fine Communications
Two Lincoln Square
60 West 66th Street
New York, NY 10023

Library of Congress Catalog Card Number 99-74461
ISBN 1-56731-354-X

INTRODUCTION

You know that bumper sticker that says "S* * T HAPPENS"? Notice, it conveniently omits the fact that for s* * t to happen, somebody or something has to s* * t.

In that spirit, *Every Excuse in the Book* is a confirmation of what we always secretly suspected: Nothing is our fault. There's really no misdeed a person can commit for which the responsibility can't be disavowed, dismissed, rejected, shifted, neutralized, sidestepped, dodged, redirected, or defused. Blame isn't something that falls on someone; it's a fly to be shooed away, and only ever really comes to land on the person who's not resourceful enough to avoid it.

With this book of excuses for any occasion, one need never be that person!

Once upon a time, blame could only credibly be shifted to another person: "He did it!" But now there are many more options. Major corporations, society, genetic quirks, food additives, governments, and even vague philosophical concepts are ready scapegoats. Not only will people accept the most flamboyant blame-shifts without batting an eye; chances are they will applaud the shifter and even name syndromes for him/her.

The proper excuse at the proper time can do wonders for the self-esteem, especially if one uses it often enough that one actually begins to believe it.

It's the Golden Age of Blame, without the gilt!

Every Excuse in the Book

My computer crashed.

It's my time of the month.

I went to public school.

My answering machine was on the blink.

I have low self-
esteem.

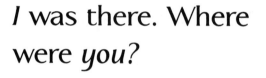

I was there. Where
were *you?*

I have an evil twin.

Newt.

You should have
been more specific.

There's no evidence
of wrongdoing on
my part.

I think I ate some bad sushi.

You should be
more accepting.

Genetics.

I was drunk.

I was testing you.

Every Excuse in the Book

It was a cry for
attention.

❧

Let's wait until we
have all the facts.

❧

In my homeland
this is acceptable
behavior.

I'M LATE

Car wouldn't start.

☉

I thought it was a holiday.

☉

My watch was slow.

☉

Every Excuse in the Book

My alarm didn't go off.

I didn't want to look too eager.

Haste makes waste.

I thought time was on my side.

I was at the right time in the wrong place.

My doctor told me to slow down.

Every Excuse in the Book

My cat got sick.

What difference
will it make a
hundred years
from now?

The lights were
against me.

I like to make an entrance.

I thought you were
being approximate.

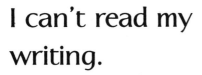

I can't read my
writing.

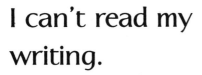

I'm on the Roman
calendar.

Road construction.

〇

My VCR just blinks 12:00.

〇

Oh! I thought it was "fall forward and spring back!"

Every Excuse in the Book

I have a slow
metabolism.

I was in my zone.

You wouldn't
believe the line at
the McDonald's
drive-thru.

I'm only human.

I was possessed by
a demon.

You must be think-
ing of someone
else.

I'm on medication.

Hillary.

I got sucked in by
a cult.

Your standards are
too high.

You're projecting.

I don't recall.

⟲

There was a full moon—or at least, a pretty full moon.

⟲

It was just one of those things.

No comment.

❀

I had a brainfart.

❀

It was the alien
experiments.

❀

Peer pressure.

Fingerprints can be faked.

Every Excuse in the Book

This isn't what it
looks like.

I haven't been
getting enough
minerals.

I just wanted to
see if you'd notice.

WORK

WORK

That kind of work
is beneath me.

◎

You should have
trained me better.

◎

That's not how you
told me to do it the
first time.

Every Excuse in the Book

I have a fear of
success.

WORK WORK WORK WORK WORK WORK WORK WORK

It's Monday.

I haven't had my coffee.

I just work here.

I need a vacation.

I'm a follower, not
a leader.

◎

These office colors
are not conducive
to productivity.

◎

I'm a leader, not a
follower.

Every Excuse in the Book

WORK WORK WORK WORK WORK WORK WORK WORK

Technology was against me.

❡

The copier was jammed.

❡

I was busy sorting out other people's messes.

It's the system.

❧

I'm inexperienced.

❧

That's how we did
it at my old job.

❧

I'm ahead of my time.

Every Excuse in the Book 29

WORK WORK WORK WORK WORK WORK

Simon said!

You're hallucinating.

The voices in my
head said to do it.

It's all relative.

I was just trying
to fit in.

You're too sensitive.

My enthusiasm got
the best of me.

My underwear cut
off the blood flow
to my brain.

Every Excuse in the Book

It was my bio-
rhythms.

I was confused.

I'm crazy.

You're crazy.

POLITICS AS USUAL

It was the vast right-wing conspiracy.

◎

I'm proud of what I did and I'll never do it again.

◎

Gridlock.

Every Excuse in the Book

The press is demo-
nizing me.

☙

Trickle-down
economics.

☙

Pork barrel spend-
ing.

Big government.

Every Excuse in the Book

Contract on America.

※

I didn't know it
was a fund-raiser.

※

My mind was on the
black helicopters.

※

"Read my lips: Oops!"

Every Excuse in the Book

G. Gordon Liddy masterminded the whole thing.

◎

Partisan politics.

◎

I was hyper from all those White House coffees.

Every Excuse in the Book

They knew what I was like when they voted for me.

⟲

Everything fell into the paper shredder.

⟲

The polls indicate that nobody cares anyway.

Every Excuse in the Book

It's a crazy world.

Any reasonable
person would have
done the same
thing.

I'm no rocket
scientist.

DNA is not reliable.

Statistically it was
bound to happen
sooner or later.

You should have
known better than
to ask me.

Three words:
Attention Deficit
Disorder.

I BROKE MY DIET

I eat when I'm stressed.

I'm big boned.

This candy bar is just to give me the energy to exercise.

Every Excuse in the Book

I BROKE MY DIET I BROKE MY DIET I BROKE MY DIET I BROKE MY DIET

I need to reward
myself for being
so good.

⊙

Gramps ate bacon
every morning and
lived to be 103.

⊙

Every Excuse in the Book

I might get hit by a bus tomorrow.

I'll work it off later.

Those damn sub-liminal messages in food advertising.

French fries are vegetables.

The diet soda
balances it out.

Everything is okay
in moderation.

It was taste tempt-
ing.

I have the fat gene.

It would have gone stale.

I'm on a low-impact diet.

That pie was call-
ing to me.

Every Excuse in the Book

Wires got crossed.

There was an
unfortunate misun-
derstanding.

I'll look into it and
get back to you.

It was creative
problem-solving.

I just have one of
those "guilty
faces."

You're paranoid.

You know I'm an idiot.

Could it be a gas leak?

I was adopted.

It was meant to be.

It's society's fault.

You mean this isn't
a dream?

I got caned in
Singapore.

I'm a Capricorn.

I'm no mind reader.

⟲

I haven't been
getting enough
sleep.

⟲

You have a bad
attitude.

I got a wild hair.

THE SEXES

You're from Mars;
I'm from Venus.

Every Excuse in the Book

I was in my cave.

*

My wave crashed.

*

I have a headache.

*

I thought you'd
think it was sexy.

Every Excuse in the Book

It was the heat of
the moment.

◎

I was blinded by
passion.

◎

It's not a fault, it's
a fetish.

Performance
anxiety.

◉

This is just how
men/women are.

◉

My crotch does all
my thinking.

Every Excuse in the Book

I misread the manual.

Every Excuse in the Book

It wasn't in *The Rules.*

⊙

Love makes you do funny things.

⊙

I'm messed up from reading self-help books.

Every Excuse in the Book 63

Estrogen.

I'm lovesick.

Imperfections are endearing.

Testosterone.

I'm not Superman.

◎

I'm not Wonder
Woman.

◎

I'm cute enough to
get away with it.

◎

Every Excuse in the Book

I'm the oldest child.

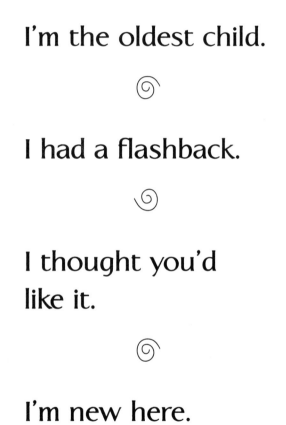

I had a flashback.

I thought you'd
like it.

I'm new here.

You misinterpreted
it.

⊚

You drove me to it.

⊚

I didn't know what
I was doing.

⊚

Every Excuse in the Book

The CIA planted a microchip in my brain.

I was set up.

⟲

Photos can be
faked.

⟲

You put the worst
possible spin on
things.

Don't you trust me?

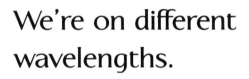

We're on different wavelengths.

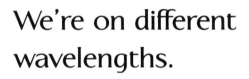

I'm rubber and you're glue.

I never adjusted to
daylight saving
time.

⊚

Who among us
is completely inno-
cent?

⊚

Nobody's perfect.

All the other kids
are doing it.

It was my imagi-
nary friend.

I got orders from
Barney.

Every Excuse in the Book

KIDS KIDS KIDS KIDS KIDS KIDS KIDS KIDS

I missed my nap
time.

෴

I didn't mean noth-
ing by it.

෴

He kept looking at
me.

I was just playing.

🌀

Normie's mom lets
him do it.

🌀

She took my turn.

🌀

I'm just being a kid.

Every Excuse in the Book

KIDS KIDS KIDS KIDS KIDS KIDS KIDS KIDS

I wasn't trying to
break anything.

◎

I don't know why, I
just did it.

◎

My mom said I
could.

He made me do it.

Every Excuse in the Book

I do that all the time.

She did it first.

It was dead when I found it.

KIDS KIDS KIDS KIDS KIDS KIDS KIDS

I don't know.

He deserved it.

I just did it to bug you.

Every Excuse in the Book

You're being judgmental.

I'm an only child.

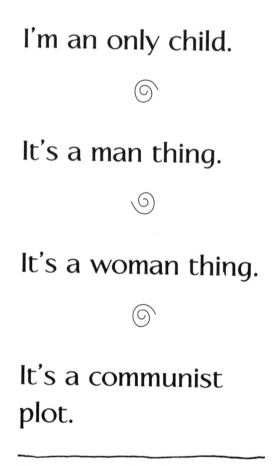

It's a man thing.

It's a woman thing.

It's a communist plot.

Sugar rush.

〇

I called, but your
phone's always
busy.

〇

Your thinking is too
limited.

I never had a pet.

Bad times help us
appreciate the
good times.

You never told me
not to.

I was double-dog
dared.

The teacher hates me.

I thought slackers were still in.

I have raging hormones.

Every Excuse in the Book

SCHOOL SCHOOL SCHOOL SCHOOL SCHOOL

I thought this was study hall.

🌀

I'm not fluent in ebonics.

🌀

The tests are ethnically biased.

I'll never need this in the real world.

I'm a latchkey kid.

There are no jobs out there anyway.

Every Excuse in the Book

I have problems at home.

⊙

I need a miracle to pass and you won't let me pray.

⊙

I forgot my cheat sheet.

Every Excuse in the Book 87

Kurt Cobain.

◎

The cafeteria food
made me delirious.

◎

I drank a slushy
too fast and it
froze my brain.

I'm tired from playing midnight basketball.

I was trying to remember where I left my gun.

Teen angst.

I'm Gen X.

I have hemorrhoids.

۞

The government
shutdown.

۞

Ronald Reagan.

۞

I was hypnotized.

I got bad advice.

...   ...

I don't get paid
enough to put that
kind of effort out.

🌀

How do you know
it was me?

🌀

I didn't want to
seem too perfect.

You're thinking in black and white. Think in shades of gray.

⟲

This is normal behavior for an extremist.

⟲

I was within
an acceptable
arbitrary margin
of error.

⊙

I'm just doing my
best.

⊙

I'm perfect.

The Psychic Network lied to me.

I was following my
instincts.

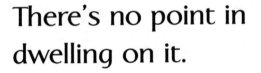

There's no point in
dwelling on it.

You're a perfec-
tionist.

SPEED TRAP

My accelerator's stuck.

○

My wife's about to have a baby.

○

I've got to catch a plane.

Every Excuse in the Book

I really, really have
to use the bath-
room.

⊚

I'm late for work.

⊚

My speedometer's
busted.

I had a touch of road rage.

◎

I was just keeping up with the flow of traffic.

◎

Some psycho was chasing me.

I thought you wanted to race.

You wouldn't want
me to miss Oprah!

◎

I keep forgetting
I'm not in Montana.

◎

I was trying to get
out of your way!

Every Excuse in the Book

I thought that speed limit was in kilometers.

꩜

It was downhill.

꩜

I had to get there before I ran out of gas.

Every Excuse in the Book

Blame Christopher Columbus.

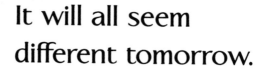

It will all seem different tomorrow.

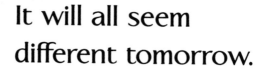

Someday you'll understand.

You're not seeing the humor in it.

You get what you pay for.

Ozone.

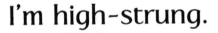

I'm high-strung.

Rap music.

It was a cry for
help.

॰

Why wasn't there
a warning label?

॰

It's not a perfect
world.

I come from bad stock.

You're prejudiced
against people who
screw up.

＊

I'm nursing a
broken heart.

＊

Everyone's entitled
to one mistake.

THE DOCTOR'S OFFICE

Those nurses are always handing me the wrong tools.

Every Excuse in the Book

I *did* it right. You're not *healing* right.

⟲

Sure, you'd get better and then what? I'd never see you again.

⟲

Your case is unique.

The "Dr." is just an honorary title.

⟲

If you think this is easy you should try it.

⟲

It was that *other* guy in the mask.

Every Excuse in the Book

Why do you think they call it a "practice"?

Ⓢ

I get woozy at the sight of blood.

Ⓢ

You don't really need that organ.

It's these cheap scalpels they make us use.

⚲

The medical journals needed a good story.

⚲

It worked on *ER*.

I just scrubbed up and didn't want to get my hands all messy.

I did everything I could that your insurance would cover.

That Hippocratic
Oath only applies
to hippos.

Who's the doctor,
me or you?

Guts are gross!

Every Excuse in the Book

I was in over
my head.

☺

I don't understand
it myself.

☺

I thought you
wanted me to.

Backward masking.

In a strange way I
did it to show you I
love you.

⟲

The line between
right and wrong is
very thin.

⟲

I'm not a god.

Why didn't you
stop me?

I couldn't help
myself.

I took a chance.

Every Excuse in the Book

I haven't been the same since Elvis died.

I thought you were
kidding.

🌀

I was role playing.

🌀

I have a short
attention span.

🌀

I'm the bad seed.

I was seduced by
the dark side of
the Force.

I was in heat.

It was fresh yester-day.

Every Excuse in the Book

We like to keep the
health officials on
their toes.

Of course it's moving. It's packed with vitamins.

〇

Hair is protein.

〇

You're the first person to complain.

This isn't my table.

🌀

I just serve it, I
don't cook it.

🌀

We're shorthanded.

🌀

New chef!

RESTAURANT RESTAURANT RESTAURANT RESTAURANT

It's an old family recipe.

◎

It's your taste buds.

◎

It's the atmosphere.

◎

It won't kill you.

☺

There's no accounting for taste.

☺

Are you trying to stiff me on the tip?

If I didn't, some-
body else would
have.

۵

I was just kidding.

۵

Temporary insanity.

۵

It was the caffeine talking.

I blacked out—
what happened?

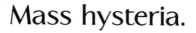

Mass hysteria.

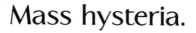

I'm a conscientious
objector.

It was civil disobe-
dience.

Peer pressure.

Life's just funny
that way.

I'm the middle child.

Every Excuse in the Book

It's all part of the grand scheme of things.

I was caught up in forces I don't understand.

I was tired.

The umpire is senile.

My jock was too tight.

It hasn't been the same since the baseball strike.

Every Excuse in the Book

SPORTS SPORTS SPORTS SPORTS SPORTS SPORTS

The sun was in my eyes.

SIZZLE!

SPORTS SPORTS SPORTS SPORTS SPORTS SPORTS SPORTS

I felt sorry for the other team.

⊚

My mind was on endorsement deals.

⊚

It hasn't been the same since instant replay.

I snapped.

SPORTS SPORTS SPORTS SPORTS SPORTS SPORTS

I swallowed too much tobacco juice.

🌀

When you win, the fans tear up your city.

🌀

Those guys are good!

Every Excuse in the Book

I chose the wrong
role models.

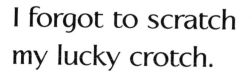

I forgot to scratch
my lucky crotch.

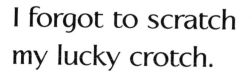

Someone switched
my Gatorade with
'gator pee.

SPORTS SPORTS SPORTS SPORTS SPORTS SPORTS

Payola, obviously.

◎

That fire in my
belly was just gas.

◎

I keep remembering
Roseanne doing
the national
anthem.

Every Excuse in the Book

I got a cramp from signing autographs.

I got realigned.

It's only a game.

Steinbrenner!

Every Excuse in the Book

I haven't been myself lately.

It's bigger than
both of us. Or at
least, me.

⟲

I was a victim of
circumstances.

⟲

I was passion's
plaything.

I cleared it with my lawyer.

It was a momen-
tary lapse.

I wouldn't have
done it if I had
known it was illegal.

My mind was else-
where.

It's a syndrome.

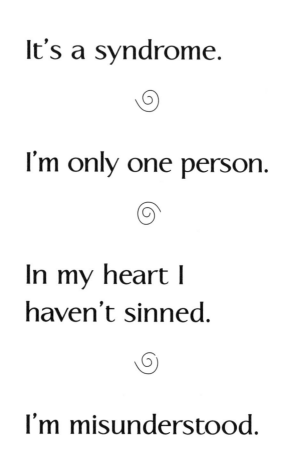

I'm only one person.

In my heart I
haven't sinned.

I'm misunderstood.

I only have two hands.

My convergence wasn't harmonized.

My crystal was cloudy.

Somebody changed my channeler.

My chakras are
clogged.

Every Excuse in the Book

I'm not centered today.

◎

Too much "Dia," not enough "netics."

◎

I was in an alpha state.

Every Excuse in the Book

I'm homeopathetic.

〇

My aromatherapist stinks!

〇

My third eye was bloodshot.

〇

NEW AGE NEW AGE NEW AGE NEW AGE NEW AGE

It was part of a
pagan ritual.

◎

My angel told me
to do it.

◎

I was having an
OBE—"Out of
Brain Experience."

Every Excuse in the Book

I haven't had my colon cleansing this week.

⟳

I'm under a lot of accupressure.

⟳

Bad Feng Shui.

NEW AGE NEW AGE NEW AGE NEW AGE NEW AGE

Those laws don't apply to me.

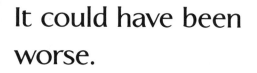

It could have been worse.

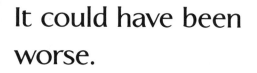

I had an overbear-ing father.

Every Excuse in the Book

What is truth?

⟲

I had an overpro-
tective mother.

⟲

C'est la vie.

⟲

God told me to.

That's the way I interpreted it.

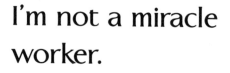

I'm not a miracle worker.

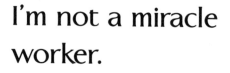

You can't blame a porcupine for being pointy.

My mind wandered.

That's ancient
history.

🌀

Don't sweat the
small stuff.

🌀

The buck stops
over there some-
where.

You call this a prob-
lem? The Titanic.
Now there was a
problem!

❀

You're persecuting
me.

❀

You sure are picky.

Every Excuse in the Book   161

THE FINAL FRONTIER

I didn't want to screw with the Prime Directive.

◎

I stood too close to the dilithium crystals.

◎

I'm only an android.

Every Excuse in the Book

I thought this was
the holodeck.

◎

You didn't say
"Make it so."

◎

The engines coulnna'
take anymore!

Part of my brain didn't beam up.

Every Excuse in the Book

I've been assimilated.

I'm part Romulan.

My mind was melded.

My emotion chip overloaded.

THE FINAL FRONTIER THE FINAL FRONTIE

Warp speed makes me nauseated.

Every Excuse in the Book

Blame "Q".

Ⓖ

You're a Picardi, I'm
a Kirkite.

Ⓖ

I never claimed to
be an intelligent
life-form.

It was a reflex.

Every Excuse in the Book

You can't blame a
guy for trying.

🌀

You're seeing the
cup as half empty.

🌀

Most people love
that about me.

I've always been
unpredictable.

I had one of my
spells.

I was caught up in
the moment.

It was my clone.

It's the times we're living in.

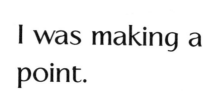

I was making a point.

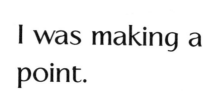

I'm in great pain.

Geniuses are often
unappreciated.

You're lucky I did
this well.

Poor potty training.

You just don't get it, do you?

I'm having a bad hair day.

I didn't eat my Wheaties.

I learned it from TV.

HUG A TREE

I have oil slicks on the brain.

◎

It was the kanga-roo rat in me.

◎

I was on a Rocky Mountain High.

Every Excuse in the Book

My brain cells are an endangered species.

◎

I'm worried about the beaver.

◎

I've got dry rot.

Got a touch of the ol' Lyme disease.

Every Excuse in the Book

I ate too many pinecones.

☺

I'm ecologically unbalanced.

☺

I was daydreaming about Forrest Tucker.

HUG A TREE HUG A TREE HUG A TREE HUG A TREE

I see spotted owls
before my eyes.

I'm an environmental
case.

All the fresh air
was getting to me.

Every Excuse in the Book

It's hard to func-
tion properly when
you're infested
with chiggers.

〰

I ozoned out.

〰

HUG A TREE HUG A TREE HUG A TREE HUG A TREE

I drank milk after
the expiration date.

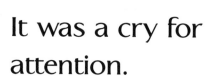

It was a cry for
attention.

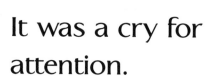

I'm working through
some issues.

I was trying some-
thing different.

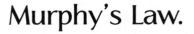

Murphy's Law.

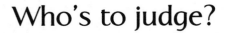

Who's to judge?

It's a victimless crime.

My dog ate it.

The weight of the world is on my shoulders.

⊙

I'm easily influenced.

⊙

Bad karma.

⊙

You're just out to get me.

I didn't want to make everyone else look bad.

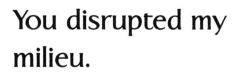

You disrupted my milieu.

It was the planetary alignment.

Every Excuse in the Book

MORE WORK

I have my own little system.

⊙

I'm breathing everybody else's germs.

⊙

This is part of a long-range plan.

Every Excuse in the Book

It wasn't covered
by our mission
statement.

⟲

This cubicle makes
me claustrophobic.

⟲

You're not seeing
the big picture.

MORE WORK MORE WORK MORE WORK

Someone's trying to make me look bad.

◎

I'm a visionary.

◎

You're not being a team player.

Every Excuse in the Book

Didn't you get my memo?

🌀

I never got the memo.

🌀

It wasn't in my job description.

Every Excuse in the Book

I didn't want to look like an ass kisser.

Every Excuse in the Book

I'm a maverick.

⟲

The low morale got
to me.

⟲

I'm empowered,
but not *that*
empowered.

Every Excuse in the Book

MORE WORK MORE WORK MORE WORK MORE WORK

Oh, you wanted
that *today?*

Management.

I'm working
smarter, not harder.

MORE WORK MORE WORK. MORE WORK

194   *Every Excuse in the Book*

I'm undisciplined.

⟳

I grew up on
Saturday morning
cartoons.

⟳

That cigarette-
smoking camel!

Asbestos.

༄

I'm a product of my environment.

༄

I was overwhelmed.

༄

My nerves are shot.

I can't operate
under that kind of
pressure.

It was a train
wreck waiting to
happen.

Sometimes life
throws you a
curve.

I have jet lag.

I'm going through
a phase.

My parents never
encouraged me.

Allergies drove me
nuts.

My inner child made me do it.

Every Excuse in the Book

This is what
happens when I
don't consult my
astrologer.

The government
hasn't banned it.

Luck of the draw.

That's not a bug, it's a feature.

✆

They don't build these like they used to.

✆

Planned obsoles-cence.

SERVICE DEPARTMENT SERVICE DEPARTMENT SERVICE DEPARTMENT SERVICE DEPARTMENT

The head office
messed up.

⊚

That noise is
normal.

⊚

It's a money
guzzler.

It's very technical.

These things are temperamental.

Have kids been using this?

Every Excuse in the Book

You should have
bought the service
agreement.

↻

You expect too
much.

↻

It's foreign made.

Ever see the movie *Christine?*

◎

I get time and a half for sitting on my butt.

◎

I don't think it likes you.

SERVICE DEPARTMENT SERVICE DEPARTMENT SERVICE DEPARTMENT

I'm old.

🌀

I'm young.

🌀

It's the darndest
thing.

🌀

I'm a victim.

I must have been a
creep in a past life.

I was sleepwalking.

Chemical imbalance.

Nerves.

I didn't ask to be born.

The altitude affects
me.

〰️

You hate me 'cause
I'm beautiful.

〰️

I had to get it out
of my system.

I had a headache.

I like to keep you
on your toes.

I'm freewheeling.

Preservatives.

I wasn't focused.

BRUSH WITH THE LAW

It was just sitting there.

The stocking on my face is to keep mosquitoes off.

◎

No one said I couldn't take it.

◎

Isn't stealing legal during a riot?

Every Excuse in the Book

If I don't steal, how can I get the money to buy drugs?

🌀

Nixon ordered me to.

🌀

VCRs are expensive!

Sure, I entered, but I didn't break any-thing.

◎

Honest, officer, I thought this was my house!

◎

I'm the anti-Santa.

I found this stuff
and I'm bringing it
back.

🌀

Their insurance will
cover it.

🌀

I'm keeping cops
employed.

Every Excuse in the Book

Armed robbery? I was just selling him this gun.

◎

I didn't know stealing was a crime in this state.

◎

It was shiny.

Social mores are
changing.

⟲

I don't know what
I'm doing.

⟲

I was exercising my
right to free
expression.

I misplaced my moral compass.

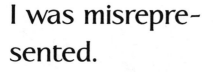

I was misrepre-
sented.

You're hyper-
sensitive.

Cell phone microwaves cooked my brain.

Every Excuse in the Book

It's in my blood.

I'm addicted to the Internet.

I was starstruck.

Force of habit.

It's just one of
those days.

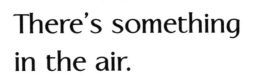

There's something
in the air.

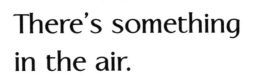

I've got a unique
value system.

There was a
communications
breakdown.

I had a momentary lapse.

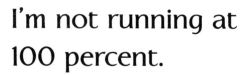

I'm not running at 100 percent.

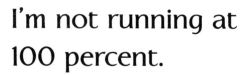

I've been staring at the computer screen too long.

I haven't eaten all
day.

It was an accident.

Entropy.

Gremlins.

SELF-HELPLESS

I needed to know it, but I didn't learn it in kindergarten.

*

I love too much.

*

I learned the wrong seven habits.

Every Excuse in the Book

I got severe tire damage on the road less traveled.

I went through the wrong twelve steps.

⊚

I'm hooked on phonics.

⊚

My higher self was feeling low.

Every Excuse in the Book

The chicken soup
for my soul was
contaminated with
E. coli.

☺

I'm okay. . . . You're
nuts.

☺

I'm disfuncted up.

Every Excuse in the Book

Someone slipped
me some bad affir-
mations.

◎

"L. Ron Hubbard?"
I've been reading
"Old Mother
Hubbard"!

◎

SELF-HELPLESS SELF-HELPLESS SELF-HELPLESS

I'm one of those good people bad things happen to.

When you run with the wolves, you step in wolf doo-doo.

I was light-headed.

Every Excuse in the Book

I'm overcome with grief.

⊚

I had a bad experi-ence once.

⊚

It was performance art.

I have a toothache.

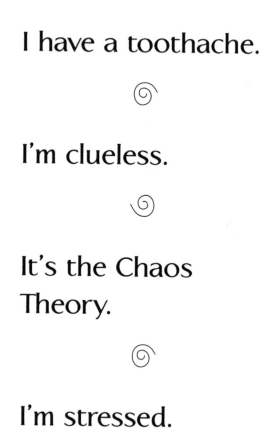

I'm clueless.

It's the Chaos
Theory.

I'm stressed.

There are two sides
to every story.

There was no
warning label.

Garbage in,
garbage out.

It was an adrena-
line rush.

I had a bug up my
butt.

◎

I was in one of my
moods.

◎

I come from a family
of postal workers.

AREA 51

It was a crash-test dummy.

୭

It was a weather balloon.

୭

All that brain prob-ing is enough to confuse anyone.

Every Excuse in the Book

It was marsh gas.

॰

Why don't you have
a close encounter
with a clue?

॰

We just like to do
autopsies on skinny,
big-headed guys.

Every Excuse in the Book

It was the planet
Venus.

◎

It was a hubcap on
a string.

◎

You're UFO: Unbe-
lievably Friggin'
Obtuse.

It was a glow-in-the-dark Frisbee.

Mass hypnosis.

You're drunk.

It was a hoax by
the FOX network.

Three letters: SFX.

It was a low-flying plane.

⟲

It was the Stealth Bomber.

⟲

I got your big cigar-shaped object right here!

AREA 51 AREA 51 AREA 51 AREA 51 AREA 51 AREA 51 AREA 51

I was affected by
secondhand smoke.

I get confused easily.

I got up on the
wrong side of the
bed.

I lost control.

I have a death
wish.

◎

I'm in a period of
transition.

◎

I was teased by the
other kids in grade
school.

In the words of John Lennon, "My mind is on the blink."

I'm thick.

I've taken a lot of shots to the head.

It's just a run of bad luck.

Every Excuse in the Book

I'm disoriented.

It's a quirk.

I'm easily influenced.

I'm a flake.

Every Excuse in the Book

It's one for *The X-Files.*

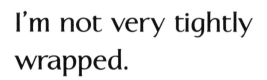

I'm not very tightly wrapped.

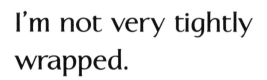

I thought this was just the rehearsal.

I was a puppet of
fate.

I COULD'VE BEEN SOMEBODY BUT . . .

I never owned a pair of $200 sneakers.

I was a day care baby.

Bad mojo.

Every Excuse in the Book

It wasn't in the stars.

I COULD'VE BEEN SOMEBODY BUT . . . .

I COULD'VE BEEN SOMEBODY BUT . . .

I never got an "I was student of the month" bumper sticker.

◎

I didn't have the proper motivation.

◎

"The Man."

Every Excuse in the Book

I was an under-
privileged child.

𝄢

I never had an Elmo
doll.

𝄢

My mom used to
walk me on a
leash.

Every Excuse in the Book   257

People hate the rich.

◎

It's a male-dominated world.

◎

My parents always liked my brother best.

Every Excuse in the Book

I never kissed the
right asses.

✺

Glass ceiling.

✺

Affirmative action.

✺

I'm ugly.

Every Excuse in the Book 259

I COULD'VE BEEN SOMEBODY BUT . . . .

I was lulled into complacency.

I was raised by wolves.

Chronic Fatigue Syndr . . . oh, I'm too tired to finish.

It was predestina-
tion.

I had no choice.

It was chickens
coming home to
roost.

I'm wrestling with my inner demons.

It's been a long day.

It's a religious
thing.

Vitamin deficiency.

It's congenital.

I haven't gotten
any in a while.

I'm a bitch.

It was urban rage.

Red tape.

You and I just have
different priorities.

My blood sugar
was low.

My mother smoked
when she was
pregnant with me.

The liberal media.

Every Excuse in the Book

The new millen-
nium.

Right-wing radio.

Comic books.

Junk food.

BLAME IT ON . . . BLAME IT ON . . . . .

Foreign influence.

Sunspot activity.

Auto emissions.

The Freemasons.

Every Excuse in the Book

The IRS.

The Angry White Male.

NutraSweet.

Fluoride.

Every Excuse in the Book

BLAME IT ON . . . BLAME IT ON . . .

MTV.

The World Bank.

Unions.

Mean people.

Corporate America.

⟳

The Men in Black.

⟳

El Niño.

BLAME IT ON . . . BLAME IT ON . . . .

Multiple personalities.

Someone's put a
hex on me.

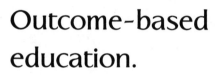

Outcome-based
education.

I've been through
a lot.

I have delusions of grandeur.

Somebody had to.

I'm absentminded.

It's my wild streak.

That evidence was
planted.

The ends will
justify the means.

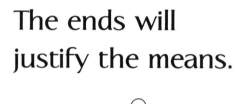

It's a defense
mechanism.

You always focus
on the negative.

Too much MSG.

Dear Abby steered
me wrong.

I'm having an off day.

I live in a vacuum.

Voodoo.

Am I my brother's keeper?

I was just having fun.

I'm not a people person.

That's life!

ABOUT THE AUTHORS/ILLUSTRATORS

Craig Boldman (left in photo) and Pete Matthews have collaborated on projects since 1978. Their words and drawings have appeared in magazines, books, advertising, and comic strips for such companies as Hallmark Cards, Gibson Greetings, American Greetings, and Disney.

Craig, a Cincinnati resident, writes the *Jughead* comic book and the *Archie* syndicated newspaper strip.

Pete is the proud recipient of Oatmeal Studios' "Most Creative Editorial" award. He lives near San Diego.

Photo credit: Ron Randall